FAMILY LAW AND PRACTICE

DOMESTIC ABUSE/VIOLENCE

QUESTIONS AND SUGGESTED ANSWERS

Written by Steve J Norton

LLB, GDL, MA, MRES, LPC

Copyright © Stephen Norton 2019

All rights reserved.

ISBN-13: 9781699346303

The right of Stephen Norton to be identified as the author of this work has been asserted by him in accordance with the Copyright, Designs and Patents Act 1988.

All rights reserved. No part of this publication may be reproduced, stored in the retrieval system, or transmitted, in any form or by any means (electronic, mechanical, photocopying, recording or otherwise), without the prior written permission of the author.

Dedicated to Barbara and Leah

Acknowledgements

I have drawn on a number of sources in compiling the questions and answers for this book. I have used relevant LPC CLP guide on Family Law and Practice as a useful source on practical application. I have also used academic texts and exam guides as well as my own exam notes to compile questions for this series of guides that will be useful for those preparing for practice exams. In addition I have also drawn on exam materials produced by the Chartered Institute of Legal Executives (CILEX) who produce extremely useful law and practice materials.

INTRODUCTION

I wrote this book as I found the subject of family law and practice very interesting when I studied it as an elective on the Legal Practice Course (LPC). I did not study this subject academically as I studied different electives in my undergraduate and post-graduate legal studies but having grown older and become a husband and a parent (slightly later in life), family law and practice seemed to become more relevant based on my own experiences. I hope those studying this area of law, and anyone else interested in how family law and practice applies in practical situations find the question and answer format useful. They are aimed at the practical application of family law rather than any attempt at academic discussion or analysis, for those starting legal practice courses. I have used a number of practical questions and suggested answers and included a few examination problem scenarios similar to those found on legal practice courses. I hope I have broken up the different elements into manageable chunks in shortish guides following the syllabus of courses like the LPC.

I hope you find these guides useful for your studies or anyone else who may be interested in learning about some of the practical steps involved in different areas of family law. In this guide I deal with the very important matter of domestic abuse/violence. The terms "abuse" and "violence" are used interchangeably.

CONTENTS

CHAPTER 1

Some key concepts

General questions and suggested answers

CHAPTER 2

Overview of legislation

General questions and answers on relevant legislation

CHAPTER 3

Orders available

General with short scenario questions and suggested answers

CHAPTER 4

Breach of orders and enforcement of orders

General questions and suggested answers

CHAPTER 5

Examples of problem questions

Questions and suggested answers

Table of cases

B V B (Occupation Order) 1999 1 FLR 715
Burris v Azadani [1995] 4 All ER 802
C v C (Non-Molestation Order: Jurisdiction) [1998] 1 FCR11
Chalmers v Johns [1999] 1 FLR 392
George v George [1986] 2 FLR 347, CA
Grubb v Grubb [2009] EWCA Civ 976
Hale v Tanner [2000] EWCA Civ 5570
Horner v Horner [1982] 2 ALL ER 495
Horner v Horner [1983] 4 FLR 50
Re B-J (Power of Arrest) [2000] 2 FLR
Re H (Contact: Domestic Violence) [1998] FLR 42
Re L (Children) [2012] EWCA Civ 2012
Re L (Contact: Domestic Violence) [2000] 1 FLR 334
Re M (Contact: Violent Parent) [1999] 2 FLR 321)
Vaughn v Vaughn [1973] 1 WLR 1159

Table of statutes

Childrens Act 1989

Criminal Justice Act 1967

Criminal Law Act 1967

Crime and Security Act 2010

Family Law Act 1996

Forced Marriage (Civil Protection) Act 2007

Matrimonial Causes Act 1973

Protection from Harassment act 1997

Serious Crime Act 2015

Bills in progress

Domestic Abuse Bill (currently being debated in Parliament (2019))

Chapter 1

Some key concepts

General questions and suggested answers

Question

Is there a statutory definition for domestic abuse?

Suggested answer

Not as such but the cross-government definition is –

Any incident or pattern of incidents including controlling, coercive, threatening behaviour, violence or abuse between those aged 16 or over who are, or have been, intimate partners or family members regardless of gender or sexuality. The abuse can encompass, but is not limited to:-

- *Psychological*
- *Physical*
- *Sexual*
- *Financial*
- *Emotional*

Controlling behaviour is a range of acts designed to make a person subordinate and/or dependent by isolating them from sources of support, exploiting their resources and capacities for personal gain, depriving them of the means needed for independence, resistance and escape and regulating their everyday behaviour.

Coercive behaviour is: an act or a pattern of acts of assault, threats, humiliation and intimidation or other abuse that is used to harm, punish, or frighten their victim. [i]

Question

Are there any changes to the definition or categories of domestic abuse to be aware of?

Suggested answer

Yes. A Bill known as the Domestic Abuse Bill 2019 aims to create a statutory cross-government definition of domestic abuse.

The definition expands the current definition to include different types of relationships, including ex partners and family members. Broader categories have been added which capture a range of different abusive behaviours. This includes physical, emotional and economic abuse. Economic abuse has been added. A factsheet has been produced at:-

https://assets.publishing.service.gov.uk/government/uploads/system/uploads/attachment_data/file/817435/Factsheet_Definition_FINAL.pdf

Regulation 33 of The Civil Legal Aid (Procedure) Regulations 2012 as amended by The Civil Legal Aid (Procedure) (Amendment) Regulations 2016 sets out the evidence needed to claim legal aid due to domestic abuse or violence.

Anyone offering legal advice should be aware of any new government legislation and changes in the law to give up to-date-advice. The Brexit negotiations has taken priority and meant implementation of this bill has been delayed.

Question

Who suffers from domestic abuse/violence?

Suggested answer

In opposite-sex relationships the majority of victims of domestic violence are woman.
According to the office of national statistics (ONS) about 4.2% of men and 7.9 % of women suffer domestic abuse in the UK during 2018. This amounts to around 685,000 male victims and 1,300,000 women.[ii] Murders related to domestic violence are at a five-year high. The majority of victims are women and the majority of suspects are men. There is still a high level of under-reporting so many cases of domestic abuse/violence may not get reported at all.

Question

How has the sociologist Antony Giddens described domestic violence in the home?

Suggested answer

Antony Giddens stated :

"The home is in fact the most dangerous place in modern society. In statistical terms, a person of any age or of either sex is far more likely to be subject to physical attack in the home than on the street at night" [iii]

Question

In terms of remedies for a victim what are the kinds of order available for domestic violence?

Suggested answer

There are two kinds of order available to a victim under the Family Law Act 1996:-

- Non-molestation order
- Occupation order

Question

Will it be through the civil law or criminal law that victims of domestic abuse can seek remedies?

Suggested answer

Victims of domestic violence/abuse may seek protection through the criminal justice system for redress from the state in imposing criminal sanctions. They may also apply for civil orders to prevent them being harassed/molested, as well as seeking occupation orders to remove someone from their home or part of it. This will be discussed in more detail in the next chapter.

Chapter 2

Overview of legislation

General questions and answers on relevant legislation

Question

Which legislation is most likely to provide remedies to victims of domestic violence?

Suggested answer

Part IV of the Family Law Act 1996 (FLA 1996)

Question

What types of order are available under the FLA 1996?

Suggested answer

NON-MOLESTATION ORDERS (S.42)

Section 42 of the FLA 1996 allows the court to grant an order that prohibits a person from molesting the applicant or a child. The word 'molestation' not only covers violence and threats of violence, but also pestering.

OCCUPATION ORDERS (SS 33 and 35-38)

These orders will exclude the other party from occupation of the home. They can be extended to exclude the other party from a specified area around the home. Occupation orders can be applied for by either spouses or cohabitants. Other `associated persons' can only apply in certain specified circumstances.

Question

Where does the Protection from Harassment Act 1997 (PHA 1997) come into domestic abuse?

Suggested answer

The PHA 1997 plugged a previous gap in the law where for example a victim was the partner of the abuser, but they had not cohabited. In this scenario they would have to bring an action for the relevant tort, probably assault. Before the Act there was no actual tort for harassment, thus an existing tort would need to used (*Burris v Azadani [1995]*[iv]). Section 3 of the PHA 1997 created a statutory tort where a person pursues a course of conduct that amounts to harassment of another and which he knows or ought to know amounts to harassment of the other. There is no actual definition of harassment apart from S.7 of PHA 1997 which states that this includes `*alarming the person or causing them distress'*.

Where a statutory tort has been committed or is apprehended, the victim may claim damages and/or an injunction. If the injunction is breached the victim may apply for a warrant of arrest, and breach of an injunction may constitute a criminal offence. This is punishable by up to 5 years' imprisonment on conviction on indictment under S.3(6) and (9).

New criminal offences were also created under the PHA 1997. This includes the offence of criminal harassment and the more serious offence of putting someone in fear of violence (ss 2 and 4 respectively). The criminal offence of stalking (S.2A) and stalking involving fear of violence or serious alarm or distress (S.4A) came in in 2012.

Section 5 gives the criminal courts power to make restraining orders that prohibits the perpetrator from engaging in further harassment if convicted of any offence. S.5A allows the criminal courts to make restraining orders on the acquittal of a defendant if they consider it necessary to protect a person from harassment by the defendant.[v]

Question

In which situations does the Serious Crime Act 2015 (SCA 2015) apply?

Suggested answer

The SCA 2015 created a new offence in 2015 under S 76 which was the offence of coercive and controlling behavior. The Act came into force in

December 2015 in order to plug a gap in the law where repeated patterns of non-physical behavior were not recognized as domestic abuse in criminal law. It only assists victims who want to make use of the police in a domestic abuse situation. The behavior by the perpetrator has to occur `repeatedly or continuously', and the victim and alleged perpetrator must be `personally connected' at the time this behavior takes place.

The behavior must have a `serious effect' on the victim. This means that the behavior causes the victim to fear that violence will be used against her on `at least two occasions', or it has a `substantial adverse effect on the victims' day to day activities'. It must be shown that the alleged perpetrator must have known that his behavior would have a serious effect on the victim, or the behavior must have been such that he `ought to have known' it would have that effect.[vi]

Question

What is the Forced Marriage (Civil Protection) Act 2007 (FMA 2007)?

Suggested answer

The FMA 2007 came into force in November 2008 and inserted a new Pt IVA into the FLA 1996 which allows a court to make a forced marriage protection order under S.63A to protect someone from being forced into marriage, or an attempt being made to force a person into marriage, or to protect a person who has been forced into a marriage. Within the order can be prohibitions, restrictions or requirements and other terms as the court considers appropriate for the purposes of the order. The order may cover conduct that occurs outside of England and Wales.

A victim can make an application or a third party such as a local authority or other person with leave of the court (such as friends, partners or even teachers of the victim).

The court will have regard to all the circumstances, including the need to secure the health, safety and wellbeing of the person to be protected, when it considers whether to exercise its powers. The court will have regard to the person's wishes and feelings (as far as it is possible to reasonably ascertain these) bearing in mind the age of the person and their understanding. It is possible to make an order without notice where it is `just and convenient' to do so, and a power of arrest can be attached to that order. Where a respondent breaches such an order this will be contempt of court and the punishment is up to 2 years' imprisonment.

It is worth also mentioning the Anti-social Behaviour, Crime and Policy Act 2014 (ASBC&P Act 2014). This Act makes it a criminal offence to breach a forced marriage protection order under S.63CA of the FLA 1996 (S.121 of the ASBC&P Act 2014) and created a new criminal offence of forcing another person to marry if a person uses violence, threats or any other form of coercion for the purpose of causing another person to enter a marriage, and he believes, or ought reasonably to believe, that the conduct may cause the other person to enter into the marriage, without free and full consent. The punishment for the offences are imprisonment up to a max of 5 years and 7 years respectively.

Question

What measure was introduced in the Crime and Security Act 2010 (CSA 2010)?

Suggested answer

The CSA 2010 introduced a 12 month pilot schemes in 2011 in Greater Manchester, Wiltshire and West Mercia police forces. Police forces under these schemes, have the power to issue Domestic Violence Protection Notices (DVPN) which require someone to leave the home straightaway for up to 48 hours, or until an application for a DVPN is heard at the magistrates' court. The police may issue a DVPN if they consider that there are reasonable grounds for believing the alleged abuser has used or threatened violence and the notice is necessary to protect the victim. The police will then need to apply to the magistrates' court for a DVPO. The DVPO will last for 14 to 28 days. The pilot scheme was extended in

2012 for another 12 months.
In 2014 the Government issued another measure to remove the need to pay court fees on applications for non-molestation orders, occupation orders and forced marriage protection orders.

Question

Is there any new legislation proposed on domestic abuse?

Suggested answer

Yes there is a new draft Bill called the Domestic Abuse Bill being debated in 2019. Details of the Bill are found on government Parliamentary websites - https://www.gov.uk/government/news/government-publishes-landmark-domestic-abuse-bill.
The Bill has been delayed due to Brexit taking priority but in summary the main points are to:-

- Introduce the first ever statutory government definition of domestic abuse to specifically include economic abuse and controlling and manipulative non-physical abuse - this will enable everyone, including victims themselves, to understand what constitutes abuse and will encourage more victims to come forward
- Establish a Domestic Abuse Commissioner to drive the response to domestic abuse issues

- Introduce new Domestic Abuse Protection Notices and Domestic Abuse Protection Orders to further protect victims and place restrictions on the actions of offenders
- Prohibit the cross-examination of victims by their abusers in the family courts
- Provide automatic eligibility for special measures to support more victims to give evidence in the criminal courts

Chapter 3

Orders available

General with short scenario questions and suggested answers

OVERVIEW ON ORDERS AVAILABLE

There are two kinds of order available for the victim of domestic abuse

NON-MOLESTATION ORDERS (S.42)

Section 42 of the FLA 1996 allows the court to grant an order that prohibits a person from molesting the applicant or a child. The word 'molestation' not only covers violence and threats of violence, but also pestering.

OCCUPATION ORDERS (SS 33 and 35-38)

These orders will exclude the other party from occupation of the home. They can be extended to exclude the other party from a specified area around the home. Occupation orders can be applied for by either spouses or cohabitants. Other 'associated persons' can only apply in certain specified circumstances.

Question

Who can apply for an order?

Suggested answer

The <u>FLA 1996</u> extended the right to apply for non-molestation and sometimes occupation orders to a wide group of `associated persons'. Section 62[vii] of the Act states a person is associated with another if:-

(a) they are or have been married to each other, or they are or have been civil partners of each other;

(b) they are cohabitants or former cohabitants (ie they are or have been living together as husband and wife or civil partners);

(c) they live or have lived in the same household, otherwise than by reason of one of them being the other's employee, tenant, lodger or boarder;

(d) they are relatives (this term includes immediate relations and other close relations such as grandparents, grandchildren, aunts, uncles, nieces, nephews, cousins, step-parents and step-children) of the applicant or of the applicant's former or current spouse, civil partner or cohabitant;

(e) they have agreed to marry or enter into a civil partnership with one another (whether or not that agreement has been terminated – however, where the agreement has been terminated, any application must be made within three years of the termination date), or they have or have had an intimate personal relationship with each other which was of significant duration;

(f) in relation to a child, they are both parents or have, or have had, parental responsibility (where a child has been adopted, two people will be associated if one is the natural parent and the other is the child or adoptive parent of the child);

(g) they are parties to the same family proceedings (other than proceedings under Pt IV of the FLA 1996 itself).

In addition to the above, children under 18 can apply for non-molestation and/or occupation orders in their own right. It should be noted if they are under 16 they will require leave of the court, which will only be given if the court is satisfied that the child has sufficient understanding to make the application (s 43).

1. NON-MOLESTATION ORDERS

General

Section 42 of the FLA 1996 allows the court to make orders prohibiting a person from molesting a person with whom he is associated and from molesting a relevant child. There is no definition of molesting in the FLA 1996. In *Horner v Horner* [1983] [viii]Ormrod LJ said, at page 51 G : *"... I have no doubt that the word 'molesting'...does not imply necessarily either violence or threats of violence. It applies to any conduct which can properly be regarded as such a degree of harassment as to call for the intervention of the court."...* Thus the word `molesting' can go beyond actual physical violence and threats of violence. Abusive or aggressive telephone calls or late night calls, emails and/or letters (and possibly other abuse on social media) may also fall into this category. In *George v George [1986]* [ix] after separation, H gave an undertaking not to assault, molest or otherwise interfere with W. He subsequently wrote a letter "in extremely abusive terms" and was formally warned that this was a breach of his undertaking and he was sentenced.

Question

Are there factors in S.42 the court must consider in deciding whether to grant a non-molestation order?

Suggested answer

Yes. Section 42(5) specifies that the court must have regard to all circumstances, including the need to secure the health, safety and well-being of the applicant and any child. Therefore, provided the applicant can show a genuine need for protection, a non-molestation order will be granted. Section 42 (7) says the order can be made for a specified period or further order. This means an order can be made for an indefinite period (*Re B-J (Power of Arrest) [2000]* [x]).

2. OCCUPATION ORDERS

General

An occupation order allows the Court to decide who should live, or not live, in the home or any part of it. The order can also exclude the other person from an area around the home. The power to make an order is contained in sections 33 and 35 to 38 of the FLA 1996.

An occupation order can also deal with who pays the rent or mortgage and outgoings on the property, who has to maintain the property, what furniture and contents can be used and whether the party in occupation should pay a "rent" to the other person.

The FLA 1996 grants the courts the power to make an order in relation to occupation of the home under ss 33 and 35-38. Occupation orders under the Act will vary based on the status of the applicant (i.e their right to occupy the home, being a former spouse, cohabitant or former cohabitant). This will determine their right to apply for such an order, the provisions of any order granted, the factors the court will consider when deciding if to grant an order or not, and the duration of any occupation order.
The application for an occupation order can either be made during other family proceedings, or the applicant can alternatively make a `free standing' application under the FLA 1996.

Question

How does S.33 work (applicant has an existing right to occupy the home) and what are the considerations?

Suggested answer

If the applicant has a beneficial estate, interest or contract or statutory entitlement (eg under S.30[xi] of the FLA 1996), in the property he/she has a right to occupy the property under this section. The home in question must be, have been, or have been intended to be, the home of the applicant and the person with whom she is associated (the respondent). So any associated person can apply under S.33 where she has an existing legal right to occupy the home.

If the above conditions are met the applicant can apply for an occupation order under S.33 which may:-

- Enforce the applicant's entitlement to enter or remain in occupation of the house or part of it;
- Prohibit, suspend or restrict the exercise by the respondent of any right of his to occupy the home, including his matrimonial home rights;
- Regulate the occupation of the dwelling house by either or both parties.

Section 33(6) provides that in deciding whether to grant the order sought, the court must take into account all circumstances, including:

The respective housing needs and housing resources of the parties and any child;

The respective financial resources of the parties;

The likely effect of any order, or of any decision by the court not to make such an order, on the health, safety or well-being of the parties and any relevant child; and

The conduct of the parties in relation to each other and otherwise.

However, S.33(6) is subject to the 'balance of harm' test contained in S.33(7). This provides attributable to the conduct of the respondent if an occupation order is not made, then the court *shall make such an order unless it appears to the court that:*

(a) the respondent or any child is likely to suffer significant harm if the order is made; and

(b) the harm likely to be suffered by the respondent or child is as great as or greater than the harm attributable to the conduct of the respondent which is likely to be suffered by the applicant or child if the order is not made.[xii]

Where an occupation order is made under S.33 it can be made for a specified period, until the happening of a specified event or until further notice. It could be possible to make an order for an indefinite period but in practice, it is more likely (initially at least) for an order to be for a specified period such as 6 months.

Question

How does the `balance of harm' test work?

Suggested answer

The court has complete discretion to make an order apart from S.33(7) of the FLA 1996. The court may feel that the applicant, or any relevant child, is likely to suffer any significant harm that can be attributed to the conduct or behavior of the respondent, if the order is not made. The court shall then make the order unless it appears to it that the respondent or any relevant child is likely to suffer significant harm if the order is made, and that harm is as great or greater than the harm which is likely to be suffered by the applicant or child if the order is not made.

Question

Are there some case examples of the application of the `balance of harm' test?

Suggested answer

Chalmers v Johns [1999] [xiii] – The applicant needed to show she would suffer significant harm attributable to the respondent's conduct *before* the court would apply the balance of harm test. Where such harm was not shown, the case would be determined on the basis of the factors in S.33(6) alone. Therefore, if the balance of harm test is made out in the applicant's favour, the court must make the order. If the test is not made out then the court has a discretion to make the order by applying the factors in S.33(6).

In *Grubb v Grubb [2009]* [xiv] the Court of Appeal refused leave to appeal against an occupation order granted in the absence of violence between the parties. The order had been made under s 33(6) as the balance of harm test was not made out. The judge found that the husband had been verbally abusive and domineering, and that both parties were suffering from stress as a result of their continuing to live together. In this case the husband was in a position to arrange alternative accommodation for himself relatively easily and the occupation order was only made for a period of three months.

In *Re L (Children) [2012]* [xv], a decision was upheld where the court found, in a case where there was no physical violence, that the children were suffering significant harm caused by the arguments between the parties, but that this harm was not attributable solely to the father's conduct, and so the balance of harm test in S.33(7) was not made out. However, the court made an occupation order after applying S. 33(6).

Question

Who is entitled to make a S.35 order (applicant is former spouse or former civil partner) and what are the considerations?

Suggested answer

Under S.35 an applicant must be a former spouse of the respondent. The respondent must be entitled to occupy the home by virtue of a beneficial estate, interest or contract based on statute. It must be the case that the home is, or have been intended to be, the matrimonial home. The applicant if they meet the above conditions, can then apply for an occupation order.

An order that is granted under S.35 must have a provision, known as an `occupation provision' which states:-

- If the applicant is in occupation, that the applicant has a right not to be excluded from the home or part of it by the respondent for a specified period and prohibiting the respondent from excluding the applicant during that period;
- If the applicant is not in occupation, that the

applicant be given a right to enter and occupy the home for a specified period and requiring the respondent to permit the exercise of that right.[xvi]

The order may also include other provisions known as `exclusion provisions'. Examples are:-

- Either party regulating the occupation of the home;
- Prohibiting, suspending or restricting the respondent's right to occupy the home;
- A provision that the respondent leave the home or part of it;
- Inclusion of a provision to exclude the respondent from a defined area where the is situated.

If an occupation order is made under S.35 it must be for a specified period which does not exceed 6 months. The order can be extended several times, but not beyond 6 months and will end if either party dies.

Question

Are there factors in S.35 the court must consider in deciding whether to grant an occupation order?

Suggested answer

Yes. The court must take into account all circumstances when making a decision whether to make an occupation provision. Factors the court must consider include:-

a) The respective housing needs and housing resources of the parties and any child;

b) The respective financial resources of the parties;

c) The likely effect of any order, or of any decision by the court not to make such an order, on the health, safety or well-being of the parties and any relevant child;

d) The conduct of the parties in relation to each other and otherwise;

e) The length of time that has elapsed since the parties ceased to live together;

f) The length of time that has elapsed since the marriage ended; and

g) The existence of any pending proceedings between the parties under S.23A or S.24 of the Matrimonial Causes Act 1973 (MCA 1973) and Sch 1 to the CA 1989 (financial orders relating to children), or relating to the legal or beneficial ownership of the home (S.35(6)).[xvii]

Question

How does a S.36 order operate (applicant is a cohabitant or former cohabitant) and what are the considerations?

Suggested answer

Section 36 applies where the applicant is cohabitant or former cohabitant of the respondent. Under this section other `associated persons' will not be able to apply under S.36. An example would be a nephew who cannot apply for an occupation order against his uncle under this section. The respondent must be entitled to occupy the home based on their rights through beneficial estate, contract or statute.
The home must be, or have been intended to be, the home of the couple.
If the applicant meets all of the above conditions he/she can apply for an occupation order.

Where an occupation order is made under S.36 it must be for a specified period that does not exceed 6 months. The order can only be extended once and this is for a further specified period that does not go beyond 6 months. This means the maximum period for which a cohabitant or former cohabitant can obtain an occupation order is **one year.** Once again the order will have no further effect on the death of applicant or respondent.

Question

Are there factors in S.36 the court must consider in deciding whether to grant an occupation order?

Suggested answer

Yes. The court must take into account all circumstances when making a decision whether to make an occupation provision. Factors the court must consider will include:-

The court must take into account all circumstances, including:-

a) The respective housing needs and housing resources of the parties and any child;

b) The respective financial resources of the parties;

c) The likely effect of any order, or of any decision by the court not to make such an order, on the health, safety or well-being of the parties and any relevant child;

d) The conduct of the parties in relation to each other and otherwise;

e) The nature of the parties' relationship, and in particular the level of commitment involved in it;

f) The length of time that they have lived together as husband and wife;

g) Whether there are or have been any children who are children of both parties, or for whom both parties have or have had parental responsibility;

h) The length of time that has elapsed since the parties ceased to live together; and

i) The existence of any pending proceedings between the parties under Sch 1 to Childrens Act 1989 (financial orders relating to children), or relating to the legal or beneficial ownership of the home (S.36(6)).

The court in deciding whether to make an *exclusion provision, must take into account all* circumstances, including the factors in the first four bullet points above in relation to an occupation provision. The court must also consider the following balance of harm questions:

(a) whether the applicant or any relevant child is likely to suffer significant harm attributable to the conduct of the respondent if the exclusion provision is not made; and

(b) whether the harm likely to be suffered by the respondent or child if the provision is included is as great or greater than the harm attributable to the conduct of the respondent which is likely to be suffered by the applicant or child if the provision is not included.

This is similar to the balance of harm test in ss 33 and 35, but there is no duty on the court to make an order where the greater harm to the applicant or child is established, it is just one question to be considered.

Once an order has been made and for so long as it is in force, S.36(13) provides that the applicant will be afforded the same protection as a spouse under S.30(3)–(6). This means that a mortgagee or landlord must accept payments towards the mortgage or rent made by the applicant.[xviii]

Question

How do S.37 and S.38 orders operate (neither party has a right to occupy the home cohabitant) and what are the considerations?

Suggested answer

S.37 and S.30 allow a spouse, civil partner, or former spouse or civil partner, cohabitant or former cohabitant, to apply for an occupation order against the other in relation to the home in which they both live or lived together but neither has a right to occupy. One example where these sections can be used is to give the applicant a licence to occupy the home owned by the respondent's parents. Section 37 applies to spouses or former spouses. Section 38 applies to cohabitants or former cohabitants. In the same way as with sections 33,35 and 36 these orders can exclude the respondent from the home or an area around where the home is situated.

An order granted under S.37/38 will last for a specified period that does not exceed 6 months. In the case where the applicant is a spouse or former spouse, the order can be extended on one or more occasions, each time for a specified period not exceeding 6 months. Where the applicant is a cohabitant or former cohabitant, the order can be **extended once only for a further specified period not exceeding six months.**

In deciding whether to make such an ancillary order and in what terms, the court shall have regard to all circumstances of the case, this will include the financial needs, resources and obligations of the parties. Any ancillary order will last for the same length of time as the occupation order itself.

Question

Are there factors in S.37 and S.38 the court must consider in deciding whether to grant an occupation order?

Suggested answer

Yes. the court must take into account similar factors to those under s 33 (where a spouse or former spouse is applying) or s 36 (where a cohabitant or former cohabitant is applying).

Question

Are there additional orders that may be made to deal with other matters?

Suggested answer

Yes. The court when making an occupation order under S.33, S.35 or S.36 can make an Ancillary order to deal with other matters such as **payment of the mortgage, repairs and other outgoings** under S.40 FLA 1996. Plus any order to pay the person excluded from the part rent, where they would normally have the right to occupy the home, if not for the occupation order. The court can also grant each party the use of the furniture.

Question

Is there scope for emergency applications for non-molestation and occupation orders?

Suggested answer

Yes. The court can make orders for both non-molestation and occupation orders without notice to the respondent (or `ex parte') where it considers that it is `just and convenient' to do so. These are emergency applications made under S.45 of the FLA 1996.

The court in deciding whether to allow the application will take into account a number of circumstances:-

j) Any risk of significant harm to the applicant or child if the order is not made immediately;

k) Whether it is likely that the applicant will be deterred or prevented from pursuing the application if the order is not made immediately; and

l) Whether there is reason to believe that the respondent is evading service and delay in effecting service will seriously prejudice the applicant or child.

Occupation orders are more rarely granted without notice, especially where they would involve ousting the respondent from his home.

Question

What is section 46 of the Family Law Act 1996?

Suggested answer

Section 46 of the FLA 1996 gives the court the option to accept an undertaking in any case where it has the power to make an occupation or non-molestation order. There are limitations. No power of arrest can be attached to an undertaking, and in a case where it would otherwise attach a power of arrest to an occupation order, the court will not accept an undertaking. Also, in the case of a non-molestation order *where the respondent has used or threatened violence* or a non-molestation order is needed in order that any breach can be punishable under S.42 as a criminal offence.

3. PROCEDURE FOR OBTAINING NON-MOLESTATION OR OCCUPATION ORDER

Question

What is the procedure for obtaining non-molestation or occupation order?

Suggested answer

Applications for non-molestation and occupation orders will be made to the Family Court and will be allocated in accordance with the Family Court (Composition and Distribution of Business) Rules 2014 (SI 2014/840).
Legal aid will be available provided that the applicant is eligible. Initial advice and assistance will be covered by Legal Help.

Question

What is the procedure the legal representative is likely to follow when obtaining a non-molestation order or an occupation order without notice (ex parte)?

Suggested answer

Firstly, the legal adviser will organize a Grant of Emergency Legal Representation. Emergency cover should only be granted for without notice proceedings where the applicant or child is in imminent danger of significant harm (that is there is a real risk that it will happen before a substantive application can be processed and brought before the court.

He/she will telephone the court to make an appointment if this is necessary.

He/she will need to telephone a process server to ensure he is at court at the end of the hearing to collect the without notice order to serve it on the respondent. The order must be served personally usually by a process server.

The representative would draft the following –

- Application within **Form FL401**

- Statement in support. This should contain details of the respondent's behaviour and

> the housing needs of both parties and financial resources. It is also important that it gives the reason why the application is made without notice. The statement must be signed by the applicant and contain a statement of truth.
>
> - Notice of issue of Emergency Legal Representation.

The court would find it helpful to see a copy of the without notice order sought (occupation order on Form FL404 / non-molestation order on Form FL404a) where time allows.

He should file at court notice of Emergency Legal Representation along with the application in duplicate, the statement in support (in duplicate) and where appropriate notice of acting.

The representative will attend the hearing before the judge, who will read the statement in support and listen to the applicant's oral evidence. Hand any draft order to the judge.

Any occupation order made will be issued in Form FL404 and any non-molestation order in Form FL404a. Where a power of arrest is attached to any of the provisions of an occupation order, those provisions shall be set out in Form FL406. A record of the hearing will be made on Form FL405. On filing, the court fixes a date for the on notice hearing, which will be inserted in a notice of proceedings (Form

FL402). The respondent must be given two clear days' notice of this date.

The representative will hand the process server over without notice order(s), sealed copy application, copy statement in support, notice of proceedings and notice of issue of Emergency Legal Representation. Ask the process server to serve these documents on the respondent personally and then to swear a statement of service in the form required by S.9 of the <u>Criminal Law Act 1967</u> so that it can be relied upon in a criminal court.

If the court has made an occupation order then there is a need to serve a copy of the application and the order on any mortgagee or landlord, together with a notice in Form FL416 informing him that he has a right to make representations in writing or at any hearing. These documents should be served by <u>first-class post.</u>

If the court has made a non-molestation order or attached a power of arrest to an occupation order, there is a need to take a copy of Form FL404a or Form FL406 to the police station nearest to where the applicant lives and a statement showing that the respondent has been served with the order or informed of its terms. The police won't exercise any power of arrest unless they have notice of it.

<u>Note</u>: the hearing without notice must be followed by a hearing on notice so that the respondent has an opportunity to put his side of the story.

Question

What is the procedure the legal representative is likely to follow when obtaining a non-molestation order or an occupation order <u>on notice</u>?

Suggested answer

If a without notice order has been obtained then a lot of these stages will have been completed.

- The legal adviser will organize a Grant of Emergency Legal Representation.
- Application in **Form FL401**
- Statement in support. This should contain details of the respondent's behaviour and the housing needs of both parties and financial resources. The statement must be signed by the applicant and contain a statement of truth. If a without notice order has been obtained, it is likely the statement will already have been drafted. Generally the same statement is used for both the without notice and on notice hearings. If however, other examples of violence have taken place there may be a need to draft a following on statement.
- Notice of issue of Legal Representation

The application and statement should be filed in duplicate, notice of issue of Legal Representation, notice of acting (where appropriate) and Emergency Legal Representation certificate (if appropriate)

Once filed, the court will fix a date for the hearing date, which will be entered into a notice of proceedings (Form FL402). The respondent must be given two clear days' notice of this date. Hand to a process server sealed copy application, copy statement in support, notice of hearing, notice of issue of Emergency Legal Representation and notice of acting (where appropriate). The legal advisor will ask him to serve these documents on the respondent personally and to swear an affidavit to confirm service.

It is important where an FL401 also includes an application for an occupation order, that a copy of the application and a notice in Form FL416 is served on any mortgagee or landlord which will inform him/her that he has a right to make representations in writing or at the hearing. These documents should be served by first-class post.

Once the respondent (and mortgagee/landlord) has been served, next a statement should be filed which confirms that this has been done in Form FL415.

The representative will prepare the draft order/s that are needed using Form FL404 or Form FL404a.

Next the representative should attend the hearing before the judge. If the respondent does not attend, service can be proved using the affidavit. The court in this case would then make an order in the absence of the respondent. Any orders that have been drafted should be handed to the judge. The judge will read any statements filed by the parties and may hear oral evidence from the applicant and respondent. If either of the parties has witnesses (e.g. a neighbour or relative), they may then give evidence. Any occupation order made will be issued on Form FL404 and any non-molestation order on Form FL404a. Where a power of arrest is attached to any of the provisions of an occupation order, those provisions will be set out on Form FL406. A record of the hearing will be made on Form FL405. The court may direct a further hearing to hear representations from any mortgagee or landlord.

The respondent must then be served personally with the order (even if he was present when it was made). The process server usually does this and should swear a statement of service in the form required by S.9 of the Criminal Justice Act 1967 so that it can be relied upon in the criminal court.

If the court has made a non-molestation order or attached a power of arrest to an occupation order, the legal representative should take a copy of Form FL404a or Form FL406 and sworn statement of service to the police station nearest to where the applicant lives.

SOME SHORT EXAMPLES OF POSSIBLE SCENARIOS

Ahmed and Isla are married and live in a house that is owned by Ahmed. Ahmed has been drinking heavily in recent months and has hit Isla on a number of occasions leaving her needing hospital treatment.

What are Isla's occupation rights?

Isla can apply under S.33 of the FLA 1996. She is married so she has a right to occupy the matrimonial home under S.30 of the FLA 1996 (as Ahmed owns the house).

Paul and June cohabit in a flat owned by Paul. The relationship has deteriorated and Paul has been violent to June and shouted at her to leave the flat. She has no job and depends on Paul financially.

What are June's occupation rights?

June is a cohabitant with no right to occupy the flat (as Paul is the owner). She would have to apply under S.36 of the FLA 1996.

Jerry and Harry both live in a maisonette which they own as a tenancy jointly. Harry has not been taking his anti-psychotic medication in recently months and has violently attacked Jerry on a number of occasions for no reason. Jerry has been scared to return home after recent attacks which have become more violent.

What are Jerry's occupation rights?

Jerry can apply under S.33 of the <u>FLA 1996</u> as he will be entitled to apply based on his tenancy rights

----

Steve and Leah <u>are unmarried</u> and currently live in Steve's sisters holiday home in Kent as they are still saving up for a mortgage to buy their first home. Steve has become very suspicious of Leah's recently enthusiasm for attending salsa lessons and thinks she has been having an affair instead. He confronts Leah with his accusations which she vehemently denies. Since then Steve has become more violent towards her not allowing her to go out and using violence towards her.

What are Leah's occupation rights?

Neither Leah nor Steve has any right to occupy the holiday home as it is owned by his sister so they are cohabitants. Leah would have to apply under S.38 of the <u>FLA 1996</u> in this situation.

Chapter 4

Breach of orders and enforcement of orders

General questions and suggested answers

Question

How is the law enforced where there is a breach of a non-molestation order or an occupation order?

Suggested answer

Breach of a non-molestation order is a criminal offence under FLA 1996 (S.42A) since 1 July 2007. Before 1 July 2007 where a respondent had breached a non-molestation order or an occupation order was enforced through committal for contempt of court. The mechanism of the use of a power of arrest attached to an order strongly affected how the respondent came to court. This stays the same in the situations with breaches of an **occupational order.** But in the case of **non-molestation orders** that are made after 1 July 2007, a breach will be a criminal offence and dealt with in a different way.

Question

How is breach of a non-molestation order dealt with?

Suggested answer

A breach of a non-molestation order is a criminal offence punishable by up to <u>five years' imprisonment</u> on indictment and 12 months' imprisonment on conviction in the magistrates' court. Section 42A of the <u>FLA 1996</u>, where a respondent breaches a non-molestation order, he will be arrested for the crime of breaching the order and can be charged and brought before a criminal court. The Crown Prosecution Service (CPS) will handle the prosecution rather than a legal adviser or solicitor acting for the complainant.

Question

How is the law enforced where there is a breach of an occupation order or an occupation order?

Suggested answer

Where the court makes an occupation order under S.47 the <u>FLA 1996</u> from 1 July 2007 (this would have also been the case before then for non-molestation orders), and the court sees that the respondent has used or threatened violence, against the applicant, (that is any associated person) or a child, then it will attach a *power of arrest* to one or more of the provisions of the order. There is only one exception to this, and that is where the court is satisfied the applicant or a child will be adequately protected without the need to use a power of arrest.

The court can attach a power of arrest to one or many of the terms of the order set out in the power of arrest. The respondent once he is arrested must be brought before a judge, district judge or magistrate within 24 hours.

The power of arrest will be drafted on Form FL406, which will set out which provisions the power of arrest will apply to. A power of arrest can also be attached to one or more provisions of a without notice order, but only where it appears to the court that the respondent has used or threatened violence against the applicant or child and that there is a risk of significant harm to the applicant or child if the power of arrest is not attached immediately.

A power of arrest that is granted by the court will usually expect to last for a similar period as the provisions of the order it is attached to (not always though). It is possible to extend this period several times if necessary.

A police officer will have the power to arrest the respondent without warrant if he has reasonable cause to suspect the respondent of being in breach of any of the terms of the order set out in the power of arrest. Once arrested, the respondent must be brought before a judge, district judge or magistrate within 24 hours.[xix]

Question

What if the court has not attached a power of arrest?

Suggested answer

In situations where the court has not attached a power of arrest, or the respondent's breach is not covered by the power of arrest, or an undertaking is breached, the applicant may apply for a warrant of arrest. In this case the applicant will need to give evidence on oath to satisfy the judge, district judge or magistrate that there are reasonable grounds for believing that the respondent has breached the order. The judge, district judge or magistrate can then issue a warrant of arrest.

Question

What are the penalties available for breach of orders?

Suggested answer

The kind of penalty available will depend upon if the respondent is brought before a judge in the county court or a magistrate in the family proceedings court.

In proceedings in the county court the judge can commit the respondent for up to <u>2 years</u> or impose an unlimited fine. In the family proceedings court, the respondent can be fined <u>up to a max of £5,000</u> or committed for <u>up to 2 months</u>. The judge will consider all the circumstances where a defendant is facing committal proceeds and whether the hearing should be adjourned for him/her to be represented.

Only in exceptional cases would immediate committal in the county and family proceedings court be used. There were guidelines set in *Hale v Tanner [2000]* [xx]. These included looking at factors, for instance imprisonment should not be an automatic response to breach of an order, the court should look at the context for instance If there are aggravating or mitigating factors, the length of committal in relation to max available and look at suspension of sentence if the if circumstances permit.

Longer custodial sentences may be given for breach of the FLA 1996 since the enactment of the <u>Protection from Harassment Act 1997</u> for wider powers for sentencing.

The judge or magistrate can attach a power of arrest if none is attached.

Question

What about applications for domestic violence under the Childrens Act 1989?

Suggested answer

When the court is considering applications under the Children Act for contact/residence they will consider carefully any incidents of domestic violence against a parent where children are involved.

The court In *Re H (Contact: Domestic Violence) [1998]* [xxi]stated that domestic violence in itself was not a bar to contact but one factor in a very complex equation. The presumption will usually in favour of contact with the child/children. However, it has been rebutted in some cases based on the specific facts such as where the father had not changed his behaviour *Re M (Contact: Violent Parent) [1999]*.[xxii]

The court in *Re L (Contact: Domestic Violence) [2000]* [xxiii]rejected any presumption either for or against direct contact in cases involving domestic abuse. The court had to balance what was best for the child's welfare (in the usual way) but needed to take account of a number of other factors. These included:

- Past and present conduct of the parties;
- The effect of violence on the child and residential parent;

- The motivation of the parent seeking contact and the case of very serious domestic violence cases, the ability of the violent/abusive parent to recognise his past conduct and need to make a concerted effort to change.

Practice Direction 12J - Child Arrangements and Contact Orders: Domestic Abuse and Harm (PD 12J)

PD 12J from the Family Procedure Rules deals with Child Arrangements and Contacts Orders where there are allegations or suspicions of domestic violence or abuse. The courts will be expected to consider at all stages of the proceedings whether there may be an issue of domestic violence, and whether to make a specific child directions order in those circumstances.

Question

Are there any human rights issues?

Suggested answer

Non-molestation or occupation orders may raise issues under Article 6 of the ECHR (you have the right to a fair and public trial or hearing). Public funding is usually not available for respondents to these orders.
Article 8 (the right to respect for family life and home) could be engaged regarding occupation orders. Courts will need to give careful consideration to the

duration and scope of these orders as interference with a person's Article 8 rights must be necessary and proportionate.

Chapter 5

Examples of problem questions

Questions and suggested answers

Problem question 1

Patrick and Mary have been in a relationship together since January 2018. Patrick moved into the flat where Mary pays the rent in June 2018 and added Patrick's name to the tenancy agreement and he has been helping pay the rent. They have no children. Until recently their relationship was fine with just the occasional disagreements that couples normally have. Mary works as a Human Resources manager part time at a small retail company. However, Patrick was demoted from his temporary middle management position in January 2019, after complaints about his rude behaviour towards some junior staff resulting in a pay cut. Since then his moods have changed and he is often impatient and short tempered with Mary and refused to pay any contribution towards the rent anymore. He has also begun to drink more heavy alcohol and become physically violent towards Mary leaving her with bruises and cuts as well as shouting hurtful personal insults, and threatened to cause her serious injury if she annoys him. Mary decided she could not take the violence and abuse anymore and when Patrick was out packed all her belongings and moved in with her sister who lived a few miles away.

She has now come to you to offer her legal advice on what she can do. She wants to know any action she can take against Patrick and if she can return to the flat which she pays rent on but not have to put up with the violence she suffered.

Suggested answer

It is important firstly to discuss funding with Mary and in particular eligibility for legal aid if she meets the criteria, which is available for domestic abuse cases. You will need to the organize a Grant of Emergency Legal Representation. Emergency cover should only be granted for without notice proceedings where the applicant or child is in imminent danger of significant harm (that is there is a real risk that it will happen before a substantive application can be processed and brought before the court).

She should be advised that she has a number of ways of seeking to both protect herself from further violence from Patrick, and be able to return home to her flat.

Under s.42 of the FLA 1996 Mary could apply for a non-molestation order which would protect her from violence, threats of violence, molestation or pestering from Patrick. The fact that she has been living together with Patrick makes them both `associated persons' (S.62 (1) (a) FLA 1996, they will be either cohabitants or former co-habitants. She would be advised to make a *without notice* application (Form FL404A) under S.45 FLA 1996 as she may be at risk of harm from Patrick if an order is not made immediately.

There is no statutory definition of molestation but there is some guidance in case law. In *Vaughan v*

Vaughn [1973] [xxiv] molestation was given wider meaning ranging from actual physical violence to nuisance phone calls. In *Horner v Horner [1982]* [xxv] it was decided that there must be a sufficient degree of harassment in order to justify intervention by the court. In the case of *C v C (Non-Molestation Order: Jurisdiction) [1998]* [xxvi] - Sir Stephen Brown P held:

'There is no legal definition of 'molestation'. Indeed, that is quite clear from the various cases which have been cited. It is a matter which has to be considered in relation to the particular facts of particular cases. It implies some quite deliberate conduct which is aimed at a high degree of harassment of the other party, so as to justify the intervention of the court'.

In Mary's situation she has been physically attacked and threatened with further violence so would meet this criteria.

The court will take into account the need to protect Mary's health, safety and wellbeing. In her case she has been subjected to physical violence and threats of further attacks so this requirement should be easily met. She may also be advised to contact the police and report the attacks which may breach the terms of the <u>Serious Crime Act 2015</u> regarding *controlling and coercive behavior* where she is being subjected to continuous behavior of this kind (definition of Act discussed in an earlier question). The <u>Protection from Harassment Act 1997</u> may also come into play (also discussed earlier).

Details of process of arranging for without notice non-molestation orders is detailed earlier in this guide so useful to refer back to.

Mary is also concerned she is not able to return to her home so you will also need to advise her on occupation orders.

Section 33 of the FLA 1996 is the relevant part of the Act. If the applicant has a beneficial estate, interest or contract or statutory entitlement (eg under S.30[xxvii] of the FLA 1996), in the property he/she has a right to occupy the property under this section. The home in question must be, have been or have been intended to be the home of the applicant and the person with whom she is associated (the respondent). So any associated person can apply under S.33 where she has an existing legal right to occupy the home.

Mary and Patrick both have a legal interest in the flat they share jointly as both their names are on the tenancy agreement. If they had been married both would have had the automatic right to live in Mary's flat and not be evicted. As they are not married Mary has to apply for an occupation order if she wants to return to the flat, and exclude Patrick.

The court would first consider if they are under a duty to make an occupation order (*Chalmers v Johns [1999]* [xxviii]).

Section 33(7) of the FLA 1996 imposes a duty on the court to make an order if it appears that the applicant (or relevant child if children are involved) is likely to suffer significant harm attributable to the conduct of the respondent if an order is not made. There is only one exception to this which is based on the courts applying the `balance of harm' test (*B v B (Occupation Order) 1999* [xxix]). This basically means the court will look at whether the respondent or relevant child is likely to suffer significant harm if the order is made and this is as great as or greater than the harm that would be suffered by the applicant through the order not being made. When applied to Mary's case it seems likely she will be subject to suffer from further harm in the form of physical attacks and threats from Patrick if she returns to flat. Balanced against this may be Patrick suffering harm by being made homeless if he has no alternative accommodation.

It should be stressed that even if the court did decide that Patrick would suffer more harm, they still have the discretion to make an order in Mary's favour. They will apply the factors in S.33(6) of the FLA 1996 as a guide in deciding whether to exercise this discretion.

The factors are:-

(A) The housing needs and housing resources of each of the parties. In this case Mary is staying with her sister but it is unclear how long this will last for. It is not clear what Patrick's situation is if he had to find alternative living arrangements.
(B) The financial resources of each of the parties.

> Mary is employed in a part time job so her income will less than full time equivalent. It is not clear what her employment status is (this would need to be clarified in your initial meeting with her). Patrick is employed although on a reduced salary and he has stopped paying towards the rent leaving Mary to struggle to avoid rent arears.
>
> (C) The likely effect of any order, or of any decision by the court not to exercise its powers on health, safety or wellbeing of the parties. Patrick has used physical violence against Mary, so she feels unable to return to the flat while he is still there. This would be balanced against the wellbeing of Patrick if the result of an order would make him homeless.
>
> (D) The conduct of parties in relation to each other and other issues. Patrick has physically attacked Mary and threatened her with more serious injuries.

The court may be sufficiently persuaded that the conduct of Patrick towards Mary is sufficient to support issuing of an occupation order. They will balance this against Patrick's housing situation if this would result in him being made homeless. They may feel Mary has a place to live and decide not to make an occupation order.

To avoid the risk of notifying Patrick her partner, applying for an *on notice* application for a non-molestation order, it would be advisable to make an 'ex parte' *without notice* application instead. This will avoid Patrick, her abuser, being made aware of the application and inducing more violence or threats of violence or abuse, until it is served on him. The courts are more likely to agree to make this order. This would inform your advice to Mary.

When it comes to making an occupation order on an ex parte *without notice* basis this could be more problematic. Mary appears to have somewhere safe to stay until an application can be made *on notice,* therefore the courts are unlikely to agree to making a without notice order in her case. Your advice to Mary based on her situation are likely to be to advise her to make an *on notice* application for an occupation order.

You would advise Mary that if a non-molestation order and/or occupation order is made, they will be in place for a specified period of time. Based on current practice this is 6 months. The courts will be keen to limit the duration of the occupation order as it will restrict one of the parties' legal rights over the property.
Patrick could offer an undertaking instead of either of the orders, but the court will not accept such an undertaking where there has been physical violence (as in this case).

Any breach of the non-molestation order constitutes a

criminal offence. However, this is <u>only after it has been personally served</u> on Patrick. Where there has been a breach of an occupation order this will not be a criminal offence, instead it would amount to a contempt of court.

Problem question 2

Mario and George are in a relationship and living together in a room in Mario's mother's house who lives there as a widow since her husband died. They are unable to afford to pay rent on a flat of their own. Mario works as a dispatch rider on a zero hours contract and George works as a self-employed personal trainer with a number of clients and earns a reasonable income. They both share the cost of food and contribute to the household bills but pay no rent or licence fee thus there is no formal tenancy or contractual agreement. They are looking for more permanent living arrangement when they have saved up enough money for a rent deposit for a flat in a nice area of London.

One day they had a massive argument over who was contributing more to the household bills. Mario accused George of not paying his way and in response George punched Mario in the stomach and head causing him to fall on the floor banging his head, and threatening to do it again if he did not shut up. Mario needed to go to A&E to have stiches for cuts he had suffered on his head. Mario is now scared of George and wants to end the relationship and get George away from his mother's home and live there himself.

Mario has come to you for legal advice. What would you advise?

Mario and George are associated persons based on S.62 FLA 1996 thus cohabitants. Mario would be advised he can make an application under the FLA 1996 for a non-molestation and an occupation order. Same sex couples (as in their case) who are living together as though they are civil partners are included under the definition of cohabitants, which covers their situation.

Mario would be advised to make a S.42 FLA 1996 application, for a non-molestation order. This would protect him from violence, threats of violence, molestation or pestering behavior from George. The action of hitting Mario causing him injury requiring hospital treatment should be sufficiently serious enough to persuade the court to make an order in his favour.

Mario would be advised to first make a *without notice* application for a non-molestation order (Form FL404A) under S.45 FLA 1996. He would need to show he may be at risk of harm from George if an order is not made immediately or George will try to evade service of the order. In this case if Mario can persuade the court that he fears reprisal from George, as they are still living together in his mother's home, if the application is made *on notice*. In these circumstances he may be able to justify making a *without notice* application.

The court will take into account all the circumstances which includes, the need to secure his health, safety and well-being when considering whether the make a non-molestation order. Mario has been subjected to a violent attack so the court is likely to grant the order, which if George breaches will constitute a criminal offence.

The complication in this case regarding an <u>occupation order</u> will be the living arrangements (both sharing a room in Mario's mothers house), as there is no formal tenancy agreement where they are paying rent. This means neither of them has any legal entitlement to occupy the property (although Mario's mum may naturally want her son to live with her).

The relevant section in the <u>FLA 1996</u> is S.38 which will allow the court to make an occupation order between cohabitants when neither of them is entitled to occupy the property (which seems to fit Mario and George's arrangement). As neither Mario or George has any contract or agreement to live in the house this section applies.

Mario could apply to the court for an occupation order against George, as an associated person. The court will have the power to make an order that George leaves the house or their bedroom or exclude him from the house and a defined area around the house. The court also has the power to order that Mario is allowed back into the room they share if he is being refused access (in your initial interview with Mario you would clarify if this is the case or not). The order will be discretionary.

- (A) The housing needs and housing resources of each of the parties. It seems George has a reasonably well paid job as a self-employed personal trainer so could afford to pay rent elsewhere if an occupation order was granted.
- (B) The financial resources of each of the parties. George and Mario have been saving up for a flat so George may have sufficient money to pay for a deposit if he had to move out of the room.
- (C) The likely effect of any order, or of any decision by the court not to exercise its powers on health, safety or wellbeing of the parties. Mario has been attacked by George so may not be safe in the future especially as George has threatened further violence against him.
- (D) The conduct of parties in relation to each other and other issues. George physically attacked Mario leaving him needing hospital treatment.

The court will also consider the 'balance of harm' test factors. In this case any significant harm likely to be suffered by Mario in being subjected to further violent attacks from George if the application is not made, is likely to outweigh the harm likely to be suffered by George if an application is not made (basically having to move out and find alternative accommodation in the case of an occupation order).

In conclusion Mario would be advised to apply for a non-molestation order *without notice* followed by an *on notice* order later.

He is less likely to be successful in obtaining an occupation order on a *without notice* basis, as both parties' Article 8 ECHR rights come into play and the court will balance this against any order made (so may be advised to apply *on notice*). The court may apply attach a power of arrest to the occupation order, if breached by George he could face being arrested and taken to court.

On the basis George appears to have sufficient funds and income to find other accommodation, the court is likely to make an occupation order against him to leave the property (and possibly stay outside of a defined area around the property). This should protect Mario from further molestation or violent attacks from George in the future.

The court has the power to make an order for a maximum period of 6 months (extended only once) which should ensure George leave the room permanently.

Index

Abuse, 1
Article 8, 59, 73
Balance of harm, 30, 31, 32, 33, 38, 66, 72
Breach, 17, 19, 27, 43, 53, 54, 55, 56, 57, 64, 68
Breach of order, 6
Children, 7, 32, 58
Civil, 13, 25, 33, 39, 70
Civil partner, 25, 33, 39
Coercive, 10, 17, 64
Cohabitants, 16, 24, 25, 39, 51, 63, 70, 71
Crime, 8, 17, 19, 20, 64
Domestic, 11
Domestic violence, 7, 20, 58

Family
Family, 1,4
Harassment, 8, 16, 57, 64
Human rights, 59
Husband, 5
Law, 5, 11, 75
Legal, 5, 11, 75
Legal, 5, 11
Marriage, 8, 18
Non-molestation, 7, 64
Notice, 19, 20, 31, 41, 42, 44, 45, 46, 47, 48, 55, 63, 64, 67, 68, 70, 73
Orders, 6, 22, 23, 59
Spouse, 25, 28, 33, 38, 39, 40

ABOUT THE AUTHOR

I have studied law for many years as a part time student and have both undergraduate and post graduate qualifications and have completed the LPC. I have worked in volunteer legal support roles offering advice and assistance in mainly employment law related roles. I currently work as an advice and information officer at the human rights and civil liberties charity *Liberty*. I worked as a civil servant for many years dealing with health policy as well as employment and collective bargaining procedures and complex personal case work. I maintain a keen interest in legal issues in particular, as well as other areas of study.

[i] Home Office, Cross-Governmental Definition of Domestic Violence – A Consultation. Summary of Responses [2012], 19
[ii] ONS Statistical bulletin - Domestic abuse in England and Wales: year ending March 2018
[iii] Giddens A, Sociology (Polity Press, 1989)
[iv] Burris v Azadani [1995] 4 All ER 802
[v] Duffield D, Kempton J, Christa S – Family Law and Practice 2017 (CLP Guides) – College of London Publishing 2017 (P.267)
[vi] Ibid CLP 2017 (P.267)
[vii] http://www.legislation.gov.uk/ukpga/1996/27/section/62
[viii] Horner v Horner [1983] 4 FLR 50
[ix] George v George [1986] 2 FLR 347, CA
[x] Re B-J (Power of Arrest) [2000] 2 FLR
[xi] Section 30 gives either spouse the right not to be evicted or excluded from the property except by an occupation order under s33-38 FLA 1996
[xii] Ibid CLP 2017 (pp.254-255)
[xiii] Chalmers v Johns [1999] 1 FLR 392
[xiv] Grubb v Grubb [2009] EWCA Civ 976
[xv] Re L (Children) [2012] EWCA Civ 2012
[xvi] Ibid CLP 2017 (P.256)
[xvii] Ibid CLP 2017 (P.256)
[xviii] Ibid CLP 2017 (P.257)
[xix] Ibid CLP 2017 (P.265)
[xx] Hale v Tanner [2000] EWCA Civ 5570
[xxi] Re H (Contact: Domestic Violence) [1998] FLR 42
[xxii] Re M (Contact: Violent Parent) [1999] 2 FLR 321)
[xxiii] Re L (Contact: Domestic Violence) [2000] 1 FLR 334
[xxiv] Vaughn v Vaughn [1973] 1 WLR 1159
[xxv] Horner v Horner [1982] 2 ALL ER 495
[xxvi] C v C (Non-Molestation Order: Jurisdiction) [1998] 1 FCR11
[xxvii] Section 30 gives either spouse the right not to be evicted or excluded from the property except by an occupation order under s33-38 FLA 1996
[xxviii] Chalmers v Johns [1999] 1 FLR 392
[xxix] B v B (Occupation Order) 1999 1 FLR 715

www.ingramcontent.com/pod-product-compliance
Lightning Source LLC
Chambersburg PA
CBHW040320220526
45473CB00009B/2502